AMAZON
FIRE TV CUBE

Advanced User's Guide on How to Set Up & Manage Your Fire TV Cube Hands-free with Alexa and streaming 4k ultra HD Movies

RICH BURTNER

© Copyright 2018 by …… All rights reserved.
It is not legal to reproduce, duplicate, or transmit any part of this document by either electronic means or printed format. Recording of this publication is strictly prohibited

Printed In the United States of America

TABLE OF CONTENTS

Introduction i

Chapter One: The Amazon Fire TV Cube .. 1

Chapter Two: How to Set up Your Fire TV Cube 6

Chapter Three: Setting Up your Fire TV Cube with Alexa 16

Chapter Four: How to Install Terrarium Tv 1.9.10 On Fire TV Cube and Other Devices 26

Chapter Five: Most Frequently Asked Questions (FAQ) 44

Conclusions 48

ABOUT THE AUTHOR 51

INDEX 53

INTRODUCTION

Amazon Fire TV Cube is a new product that evolved from a combination of two recentlydeveloped living room electronics, which are the Fire TV Media Streamer and Echo Smart Speaker. In fact, it is a compl ete blend of Alexa voice assistant and Echo smart speaker with the capacity of controlling your room and offering you a smart home experience.

It is featuring all the same content specifications typical of a Fire TV 4K and Echo devices such as Amazon Prime Video, PS Vue, Hulu, Netflix, and many others. You will notice the unique attributes of Echo's voice potentials in controlling your TV as you issue out commands from any location in your home. For instance, if you want to play, pause, and control the volume of your TV with your voice or search for films and other presentations on the television and even launch video streaming apps, this exclusive and pragmatic device comes in handy. Experts regard it as the first hands-free streaming device using Alexa voice assistant in offering you private entertaining experience.

Every day, various information keeps rolling in about the different ways of streaming media. Therefore, you need to keep updating your knowledge of the latest devices available in the technological industry. This guide will help you in mastering all you need to know about Amazon Fire TV and even the apps that can function correctly with it.

CHAPTER ONE: THE AMAZON FIRE TV CUBE

Amazon Fire TV Cube

Now, you can watch thousands of television episodes and films from Prime Video, NBC, Netflix, SHOWTIME, HBO, Hulu, and other media players using your Amazon Fire TV Cube. Reddit, YouTube, and Facebook could be accessed quickly using browsers like Firefox and Silk. Moreover, you will find out several 4K ultra HD movies and other television episodes including streaming of musicals through iHeartRadio, Prime Music, and Spotify as the case may be.

With far-field voice prompt and detection modes, Amazon Fire TV Cube is the first and foremost hands-free device that offers streaming features using Alexa. You can only turn on lights, put on your television, and play any movie you want to watch, even turn off lights by speaking to Alexa. So far it can recognize your voice because it functions with voice compatibility mode.

As I said earlier, with your Amazon Fire TV, you can watch your movie series hands-free. Experts have adjudged that it is the first streaming media device you can control and use freely with Alexa. It can provide an all in one entertainin experien ce, and you will make commands from any point in your room, and the TV turns on showing lively imageries and well-contrasted colors in your 4K ultra HD.

Your Fire TV is constructed with eight microphones and beamforming technolog y enabling the device to pick your voice from any direction. With your voice, you can manage the contents of the device, A/V receiver, regulate the power, volume, and soundbar. Furthermore, you can use voice prompts and commands in changing your satellite channels or cable stations.

Do you know that even when your television is put off, you can still tell weather forecasts for the day and listen to the news? Of course, if your Fire TV is put off, you can always listen to reports, check weather conditions, and other streaming services as Alexa is acquiring new skills. Other things you can do with your Fire TV is controlling compatible smart home devices accordingly. In fact, with the original voice functionalities of Alexa, your Fire TV is becoming more fashionable and more useful every day.

You will enjoy vividly clear pictures and distinct sound features by accessing 4K ultra HD even up to sixty focal points (fps), the clarity of sound of Dolby Atmos, with HDR. Additionally, some of the brands producing all the smart devices compatible with your Alexa Fire TV Cube are Sony, LG, Vizio, Samsung, and others. You can tune in to live broadcasts with satellite boxes or cables powered by DISH, DIRECTV/AT&T, Comcast, and many others. Because there are supported devices, it is imperative to note here that you cannot sort channels through an over-the-air high definition antenna using your voice commands alone.

Finally, your Fire TV Cube is yet to support features such as Bluetooth functionalities, multi-room music, sleep timers, calling and messaging using Alexa, and other aspects of mobile phones connectivities.

CHAPTER TWO: HOW TO SET UP YOUR FIRE TV CUBE

The Set Up Process

Before setting up your Fire TV Cube, remember that you can only control compatible devices such as A/V receiver, sound bars, and television sets. As you plan to set up your cube, first of all, configure the equipment control for your soundbar, receiver, and even the television. It will be difficult to control your satellite receiver or cable box without adding it in the equipment control settings. This could be done conveniently from:

Settings > go to

Equipment control, and **then >> go to**

Set Up Equipment.

Also, if you want to reconfigure or change the settings of these devices, then, reselect

Set up Equipment

Anyway, you will be guided by the prompts of your Fire TV Cube, which will take you through the various steps gradually. You will also be conducting tests for every completed step during the configuration processes. To follow the voice prompts appropriately, look on the TV for **onscreen** instructions, and listen attentively too. Get the remotes of your Fire TV and that of other devices you want to configure with your TV. Check and determine the ports you can connect your TV, A/V receiver or sound bar, and even the Fire TV.

During the tests and setups, you may notice that your devices are going off and on, but adjust your volume to avoid straining your ears to hear the instructions of your Alexa system. In most cases, the processes could take some time, and the tests may require several attempts before being successful.

Now, a quick look at the processes involved in setting up your Fire TV Cube.

CONNECT the HDMI and power cables inside your Fire TV Cube. Then, **PUSH** the fast-forward button on your remote control device and choose the Wi-Fi network available in your home or location. By then, the system will display a dialog box, and you will be requested to **ENTER** your **PASSWORD** and click **CONNECT**.

The system will be connected automatically, but you will be requested to **SIGN IN** or **CREATE** an account as a new user of the Fire TV Cube. You will create a **USERNAME** and **PASSWORD**, or if you are already an old user, you will **SIGN IN** into your account.

At this stage, you will **ENTER** your account passwords and sign in immediately. After entering the passwords, you will be requested to verify it by clicking on **SHOW PASSWORDS,** as this will display the words again. Now, you can click **CONTINUE**. By clicking this command, your Amazon Fire TV Cube will be registered on your name or the name you used for the registration. You will be requested to indicate if you will change your account **CHANGE MY ACCOUNT**, in which case, you are expected to answer **YES or NO**.

It is good to note here that the device automatically saves your passwords on Amazon. This is vital to ensure a quicker connection with other Alexa compatible devices. This feature could be disabled or enabled merely by connecting to

Settings > then, go to

Network >>, in the dialog box, and click on

Wi-Fi Passwords

Another vital step is to **decide on** setting or programming the device for parental guides and controls. That means, you will use a PIN to LOCK the device when you do not want your kids to access it and UNLOCK it when you want to use it, as the case may be. If you're going to launch apps, buy digital contents or other items, and even play audio-visual materials from Amazon, you will enter the pin firstly, for accessibility.

To set up this feature, go to

Settings >, then

Preferences >>, and

Parental Controls

After this process, choose to **GET STARTED,** and that will take you through the downloading of Amazon app. You can also click **NO THANKS** if you want to **SKIP** it. At this stage, you can select your streaming services, but remember that you are not expected to pay, although some will require payment before full accessibility.

Choose the type of program and services, you desire by right-clicking on **TV CHANNELS**.

TV Channels

Then, proceed to choose the television channel apps you want by right clicking on **SPORTS APPS**. Choose the sports apps you want and right click on the highlighted apps for the sports and fitness services you desire. Choose the highlighted services you want and click **PLAY**. At this stage, click on **FINISH** to complete the installation processes of your television channels and Spotify.

Now, if you want **ALEXA** to control your smart home appliances, then click on **CONTINUE.** This action will enable Alexa to control your devices. Choose from the options according to your setup and follow the instructions. In most cases, this is based on your selection of appliances. If you have a television, choose the TV option. Then, you will see a notification on the screen like "Are you using a soundbar, AV receiver, or just my TV?" Select the option suitable to you accordingly and click **NEXT**. This action will turn off your TV. At that time, click **FAST FORWARD** using your remote and click **NEXT** and **CONTINUE**. At this moment, your Fire TV Cube is set up. But, if you want to use voice control and set up your satellite or cable services, you can do it later.

You can enjoy endless streaming of movies and other TV shows with 2-Day **FREE** delivery on millions of items by **OPTING** in or out of **PRIME.**

Congratulations! You have set up your Fire TV Cube.

It is advisable, to place your Fire TV Cube about two feet away from your speakers and TV set. Additionally, you can plug an ethernet cable into the ethernet adapter of the Fire TV Cube, if you want to receive enough bandwidth for 4K content. Lastly, through the micro USB port of the Fire TV Cube, you can connect your ethernet adapter for optimal performance.

CHAPTER THREE: SETTING UP YOUR FIRE TV CUBE WITH ALEXA

Now, if you want to enjoy your Fire TV Cube using Alexa, you need to learn how to set up the device, especially where you have not done it before. What is the equipment required to complete the set up successfully? Also, what other components are in the package (the box).

Here we are going to learn how to set up the Fire TV Cube with Alexa voice assistant, the necessary equipment needed, and the way to connect your TV to the system, including how to pair the remote correctly.

The Items included in the Fire TV Cube

The Amazon Fire TV Cube comes with some items such as the Alexa voice remote, 2 AAA batteries, Fire TV IR extender, Amazon Fire TV Ethernet adapter, Amazon Fire TV Cube, and power adapter.

The Equipment Needed for the Setup Process

There is various equipment necessary for the setup process to be completed such as an internet connection, HDMI cable, Amazon account, and compatible TV.

A detailed analysis of the functionalities of these devices and why you need to use them.

Internet Connection

The device you want to set up must be connected to a wired (Ethernet) network or a Wi-Fi internet connection. Without this connectivity, it will be challenging to complete the installation and even to access the contents and other functionalities of the Cube. However, if you want to connect to an Ethernet cable, you should use Amazon Ethernet Adapter.

HDMI Cable

Male-to-male HDMI A cables are ideal for your Fire TVCube. Moreover, you should use HDCP 2.2 HDMI cable in connecting the device to a compatible television.

Amazon Account

Do you have an Amazon account? You can create an Amazon account if you do not already have one. Then, you should register your device to the account you have created. This will enable you to access the latest software, functionalities, features, and contents that can help in using the system very well.

Compatible TV

You should connect your Fire TV with ultra high-definition and high definition television sets through an HDMI input port to ensure compatibility.

The Setting Up Procedures

Before setting up your Fire TV Cube, ensure that you position the device about two feet away from television sets and speakers. Here are the steps to follow and set up the Cube successfully.

The first step is to connect the power adapter, which was included through the port designated for 'POWER' behind the Fire TV Cube. After this, you can plug the other point into a power socket. Remember that the micro-USB port should not be used as a power outlet.

AMAZON FIRE TV CUBE

Power Adapter

At this stage, you should locate the IR port and plug in the IR extender. However, this port is not for audio setups. Now, if you want to connect the devices to your television, plug one of the ends of your HDMI cable into the back of your Fire TV Cube through the HDMI port.

Now, choose the input channel you used for connecting your Fire TV Cube as you turn on the TV. You will notice a logo on the screen with an inscription and emblem bearing "Amazon Fire TV." Then, get the remote control of your device and fix the batteries by using your thumbs and exerting pressure on the arrow icon behind the remote and continue pushing it up until it slides off wholly. Fix the two AAA batteries and reposition the back cover on the remote carefully.

It is time for pairing your remote with your Fire TV Cube. After inserting the batteries, your TV cube will be paired spontaneously with your Alexa voice control remote. Sometimes, the remote may not match immediately; then, you should push down the 'HOME' button and hold onto it for about ten minutes, as this action will redirect you to the DISCOVERY MODE, where you will completely pair the remote and TV accordingly.

After all these steps, it is time to follow the onscreen instructions and hook up your Fire TV to the internet. This could be done successfully using a wired (Ethernet) connectivity or through a Wi-Fi network. You will also be requested to register your device on the Amazon account by following the instructions on the screen and connect your Fire TV Cube. If you want to deregister your device, you will also apply the same process.

Ethernet Adapter

Furthermore, if you are setting up your device initially, you should set up voice equipment control. This will help in controlling your sound bar, A/V receiver, and TV as the case may be. Meanwhile, your Fire TV Cube will be conducting series of tests for you as you progress in the installation exercise, but you need to listen to voice prompts and instructions on the screen to complete the process. Again, you need the remote control devices of your Fire TV and that of Alexa voice systems to carry out the procedures.

Conclusively, go to SETTINGS on the equipment control of the device and configure how to control your satellite receiver or cable box. Now that you have completed the setup processes, you will receive a 'WELCOME VIDEO.' It is a visual tutorial that can guide you on how to use Alexa efficiently on your Amazon Fire TV Cube.

CHAPTER FOUR: HOW TO INSTALL TERRARIUM TV 1.9.10 ON FIRE TV CUBE AND OTHER DEVICES

Terrarium Tv 1.9.10 is one of the latest Amazon Firestick apps released on May 29, 2018. It functions without a paid subscription, unlike Netflix that needs an active subscription to work. With this application, you can watch TV shows, films, and other videos and no one charges you any dime. Now, if you want to install Terrarium Tv 1.9.10 on Fire TV Cube, here is a guide on how to handle it.

There are three viable ways of installing this application on your Fire TV Cube such as installing by using ES file explorer, Downloader App, and by using Apps2Fire. Let us get a detailed description on how to handle all these installations successfully.

a. Installation through Apps2Fire

Have you installed this app on your Android smartphone? Installation through Apps2Fire is the best way to have Terrarium TV in your Fire TV Cube. Then, if you have already done this, now let us understand the procedures. On your Fire TV, turn on **ADB debugging** and **Apps from Unknown Sources.** This action can be done through **Settings**. When you click on settings, go to **System/Device**, and then, go to

Developer Options. After this, is the IP address of your first device. You can get that through **Settings**, go to **System/Device**, then click on **About**, on the drop-down menu, click on **Network**. At this moment, check at the right-hand corner, you will see your IP address.

On your smartphone, go to Google Play Store and install the original version of Apps2Fire. Launch the application on your smartphone, then go to **Setup** and include the IP address of your Fire TV.

Open the Apps2Fire app and click on "**Local Apps**" Then, you can search for Terrarium TV app. If you see it, click on **Install** option.

Immediately, it will be uploaded onto your Fire TV.

With this procedure, you have installed Terrarium Tv 1.9.10 app on Fire TV Cube device.

b. Installation by Using Downloader App

Although, many persons usually complain of their inability to find and install the Downloader app on their Apps store. However, you can install Terrarium TV app on Fire TV Cube using the following procedures.

Go to **Settings**, click on **System,** then move to **Developer Options.** Then, turn on "**Allow apps from Unknown Sources**" Now, go to Fire TV main menu and type

Downloader in the box. Click and open the Downloader app and install it. After installation, click on "**GO**" With this process, the Terrarium app will be downloaded and installed successfully.

c. Installing by Using Es File Explorer

Installing Es File Explorer requires you to go to **Search Options** on the Fire TV and type in **ES File Explorer app.** Then, you should choose the app from the search results and install it.

After installation, open the ES File Explorer app and locate **Tools** on the left sidebar and click on **Download Manager.** Check the

menu at the base of your screen and click the icon with + **New**. After this, there will be a pop-up menu with double fields. Add this information:
Path: http://bit.ly/TTV1910

Name: ttv198. Having put these details, then click **"Download Now"** and you will get the new version of Terrarium TV 1.9.10. If the download is complete, you can open the file. At this moment, click **"Install"** and install Terrarium TV on your Fire TV Cube.

How to Install Kodi 18 on Amazon Fire TV Cube

Kodi was formerly known as Xbox Media, and XBMC can help you organize and manage your files, photos, and TV shows and even live television broadcasts. Do you know that installing Kodi is easy on a computer device? Of course, you can easily install Kodi on your computer device but very difficult if you want to use it as a streaming device.

Now, I want to show you the most straightforward ways of installing Kodi on a Fire TV within a couple of minutes.

On the **Settings Menu** of your Fire TV Cube and click **Device,** if you want to access your device settings. With this, you can manage the installation processes. Locate **Developer Options** and click on **Enable Apps from unknown sources.** Experts have stated that permitting third-party applications poses a high-security threat to your device such as malfunctioning of the system, therefore, if you want to install Kodi on a Fire TV device, check for the risks against the benefits.

After taking these steps, the next thing is to **locate the free Downloader app** on Amazon Appstore and **install** it. Another way to get this app is by downloading directly from Kodi website, or any other means, you want. The operating system of your Fire TV is Android app, choose this Kodi Android app and select the 32-bit installation. In fact, most users have affirmed that this version of this application functions very well with Fire TV Cubes.

If you have completed the downloading process, the next thing is to click on **Install.** With this procedures, you can access Kodi the same way you will get other applications on the Fire TV. Most of the things you can do with your Kodi is sharing media libraries, but you can review Kodi's permissions.

Installing Stremio to Your Fire TV device

Stremio is a video streaming hub where users can watch video content from various sources like managing your library of films, live TV shows, movie series, and other media sources efficiently.

Now, if you want to install Stremio, go to **Settings** on your Fire TV Cube and click on **Device.** Then, move to **Developer Options** and click **Turn on Apps from unknown sources.** After this, return to

Home on your device and choose **Search,** you can enter **Downloader,** it will help you to install the Stremio app on your Fire TV Cube. You will see a list of apps from the menu, then, choose the **Downloader**. Tap or click on the download button to get it installed on your device.

Launch the application by clicking on the **Open** icon. After opening the Downloader, go to Browser and type in **stremio.com** and click **Go.** This action will take you to the Stremio website. Then, **Scroll down** and click on other **downloads link** and the site will open successfully. As it has begun, scroll down and click on **Stremio ApK version**, which is the one you need to have on your Fire TV Cube. Having clicked on that version of the app, it will begin to download and after the downloading is completed. You will see the installation menu. Click the icon and choose **Install.** Continue checking the process until the installation is complete and then, click or tap on the Open icon to launch the Stremio application finally on your Fire TV Cube.

With these procedures, you have successfully installed the Stremio application on your Fire TV Cube. Congrats!

Installing Pluto TV on Fire TV cube

This is one of the applications of APK APP. Pluto TV can be connected from the **main menu** of your Fire TV Cube. Look at the top left side of the device and click on the **search box**. **Type** Pluto TV in the box.

From the drop-down menu, locate **Pluto TV** and click on it.

Now, you will scroll to download page and click on download. By initiating this command, Pluto Tv will begin to download, and it will start installation too. Open the app as you click on it after the installation is completed.

If you click on the **Home** icon, you will be redirected to the **main menu**. On the main menu bar, click on apps. Then, click or Tap on **See all**. When this happens, you will be able to locate **Pluto TV** on the screen.

Installing Show Box 5.05 on Fire TV Cube

Show Box 5.05 on Fire TV Cube is one of the film and television show streaming android applications having tons of content. In fact, every streaming device ought to have Show Box fully installed and operational on it.

There are various steps involved in installing this device, such as fixing the Mouse Toggle application firstly. You will not be able to use and enjoy your Show Box if you do not have this app on your device.

Follow these steps and install your device:

Go to the **main menu** and scroll down to **Settings.** Then, click on **Device** and choose **Developer Options.** Select **Apps from unknown sources** and click **Turn on.** After this, you will go back to **Home** Screen and locate the **Search** icon. On the Search Box, type the word **"Downloader."** Tap or click the

Downloader app, as it opens, click on **Download.**

Now, you should click **"Allow"** to enable the application access your data on the Fire TV Cube. Then, click **Open** to allow the app on your device. Go on and click the **Browser** icon on the Downloader app and tap or click **Ok** button on Javascript Disabled Message.

An address bar will be displayed, then type into the box this link: troypoint.com/sb. Tap or click on **Go** icon. Wait for the file to download and click **install**. After that click on the **Done** button. At this point, you will get a notification on the screen that the app is installed.

You can go back to Downloader and tap on **Delete** icon. Click on the **Delete** button the second time. Return to the **Home** screen and locate **Apps & Games.** Scroll to the right side of the screen and tap on **See All.** After that action scroll to the bottom and click on **Show Box.** Drag the **Show Box** app to the top of your list. Then, go back to the **Home** screen and click on **Show Box** to open it.

It is good to note that if you want to enjoy Show Box, you should use VPN. Experts recommend that it is ideal whenever you are streaming with free applications like Show Box. With this app completely installed on your device, you can stream or download contents anytime.

Installing Freeflix HQ

Freeflix HQ is an app developed to offer you access to thousands of films, anime, and other television shows. The library is loaded with high-quality contents packaged in 1080 HD that you can download and watch offline.

If you want to install this device on your Fire TV Cube, then follow these three steps:

Enabling Apps from Unknown Sources on your Fire TV

Firstly, plug the Fire TV Cube to your television and turn it on. With the remote, click on **Settings** scroll down and select **Device** from the list. Now, you can choose **Developer Options.** Then, click on

Select on the remote to enable Apps from unknown sources.

Installing Downloader App on your Device

On the Home menu of your Fire TV Cube, click on the **Home** icon on the remote. Check the top left side of the screen and choose **Search Tool** button and click on it. Type the word "**Downloader**" and click on the **select** icon. Then, click on the link to install the Downloader app. This will cause the application to be installed in the **Apps and games** menu.

Installing the FreeFlix HQ app on Fire TV

At this stage, you can directly connect the FreeFlix HQ app on your Fire TV Cube by running the Downloader app, and you can highlight the address bar using the remote. Type in the link by locating it and download the APK file on the second page. Click on **Next** and click or tap **Install** on the base of the screen. After this, wait for the installation process to be completed. Then, you will get the application installation notification.

Now, you will click **Open** to launch the application immediately and click **Done** to return to the **Home** menu. Con grats! You have successfully installed the FireFlix HQ app on your Fire TV Cube.

CHAPTER FIVE: MOST FREQUENTLY ASKED QUESTIONS (FAQ)

A look at some frequently asked questions arising from the operations and functionalities of Amazon Fire Tv Cube.

a. What is Amazon Fire TV?

Amazon Fire TV can be described as a device enabling you to stream movies instantly. It functions by connecting directly to your TV using wireless internet routers like Wi-Fi.

b. Is there any subscription for Amazon Fire TV?

If you are accessing Fire TV using Netflix, you will make a one-time payment of $99 per year or $8.25 per month to become a Prime member, which entitles you for streaming movies and TV shows.

c. Does Amazon Fire TV require internet?

Amazon Fire TV requires an internet before it functions as this will help you to stream contents. Easily. The Home interface of your device will not load until an internet connection is available.

d. Can you use a Wi-Fi router and enable Amazon Fire TV to function?

Yes, you need to use a Wi-Fi wireless internet router to enable your device to function.

e. Where can I see the Fire TV Cubes to buy?

You can buy the Amazon Fire TV Cubes from the Amazon platform, Walmart, Best Buy, and a host of other retailers.

f. What are the internet speed requirements for Amazon Fire TV?

There is no specific speed requirement for Amazon Fire TV, but depending on the type of video content you want to stream, you can use at least three megabits per second for standard definition and five megabits per second for streaming in high definition (HD).

g. Do you need only Netflix to watch movies on Amazon Fire TV?

No, you will find and install other apps and channels that can give you access to watch or stream films with your device.

h. Can Amazon Fire TV be used outside the US?

Yes, there are other countries where you can access and use your Fire TV devices.

CONCLUSION

Amazon Fire TV Cube is the latest technology for streaming thousands of movies and watching live TV shows. You need to pair this device with your smart home appliances, and it functions using Alexa voice assistant enabling you to turn on lights, put on your television, and play any movie you want to watch, even turn off lights by speaking to Alexa, if it can recognize your voice because it functions with voice compatibility mechanism.

With this guide, you can configure your Fire TV Cubes using compatible devices such as A/V receivers, sound bars, and television sets. If you want to set up your device, turn it on and then go to **Settings > Equipment control,** and **Set Up Equipment.**

For you to enjoy your smart home devices, you should set up your Fire TV Cube with Alexa voice assistant but ensure it is two feet away from the television. Moreover, other applications that can enhance the functionality of your device are Kodi, Show Box 5.05, Freeflix HQ, Stremio, Pluto TV, and Terrarium Tv 1.9.10.

If you can install these apps coupled with the smart functions of Alexa in your Amazon Fire TV Cube, then you are set to be enjoying unlimited streaming of movies, live TV shows, controlling your smart home appliances by using your voice, and other fantastic features.

Rich Burtner

Thanks for Reading and Good luck!!!

ABOUT THE AUTHOR

Rich Burtner is a computer analyst and a prolific writer, with over 15 years experience. He is committed to constant research on information technology and providing a solution to problems people are facing. Over the years, his engagement in software and applications development for several organizations and individuals generally is highly admired, regarded by all as a stroke of genius. He holds a Bachelor degree in computer science and a Master degree in Business administration (MBA). Due to the nature of his job, Rich has traveled to over 15 countries and speak five different languages. Technology has modified how business is operated today, allowing you to travel around the world at the same time working. As a passionate computer Analyst, Rich enjoys providing publications to the rapidly growing digital marketplace.

INDEX

A

A/V receiver, 3, 6, 8, 24
AAA batteries, 22
access, 11, 18, 19, 32, 34, 39, 41, 47
accessibility, 11, 12
adjust, 8
Alexa, 1, 3, i, ii, 2, 3, 4, 5, 8, 11, 14, 16, 17, 22, 25, 48, 49
Amazon, 3, i, iii, 1, 2, 3, 10, 11, 12, 17, 18, 19, 22, 23, 25, 26, 31, 33, 44, 45, 46, 47, 49
analysis, 18
Android app, 33
antenna, 5
APK file, 43
applications, 32, 34, 36, 38, 40, 49, 51
apps, ii, iii, 11, 13, 26, 29, 35, 37, 46, 49
Apps & Games, 40
Apps store, 29
Apps2Fire, 27, 28

B

bandwidth, 15
batteries, 17, 22
beamforming, 3
Bluetooth, 5
broadcasts, 5, 32
button, 9, 22, 35, 39, 42

C

cable, 3, 7, 14, 15, 19, 25
cable stations, 3
channels, 3, 5, 13, 46
Check, 8, 30, 42
colors, 3
Conclusively, 25
conducting, 7, 24
configuration, 8
configure, 7, 8, 25, 48
connection, 11, 18, 45
connectivity, 18, 23
contents, 3, 11, 18, 19, 40, 41, 45
Cube, 15, 17, 18, 20, 35, 36, 44

D

Delete icon, 39
deregister, 23
Developer Options, 28, 29, 32, 34, 38, 41
device settings, 32
digital, 11, 52
DIRECTV/AT&T, 5
Disabled, 39
DISCOVERY MODE, 22
Dolby Atmos, 4
Downloader app, 29, 30, 33, 39, 42, 43

E

Echo smart speaker, i
electronics, i
emblem, 22
enhance, 49
equipment, 7, 16, 17, 18, 24, 25
Es File Explorer, 30
Ethernet Adapter, 19, 24
Experts, ii, 3, 32, 40

F

Facebook, 2
films, ii, 1, 26, 34, 41, 47
Fire TV Cube, 1, 3, i, 1, 2, 5, 6, 7, 9, 10, 14, 15, 16, 17, 20, 21, 22, 23, 24, 25, 26, 27, 29, 31, 32, 34, 35, 36, 37, 39, 41, 42, 43, 48, 49

Firefox, 2
Firestick, 26
Freeflix HQ, 41, 49
functions, 2, 26, 33, 44, 45, 48, 49

H

HDMI, 9, 18, 19, 20, 21
HDMI cable, 18, 19, 21
HDR, 4
high-security, 32
home appliances, 14, 48, 49
host, 46
hub, 34
Hulu, i, 1

I

iHeartRadio, 2
imperative, 5
input, 20, 21
installation, 13, 18, 24, 30, 32, 33, 36, 37, 43
instructions, 8, 14, 23, 25
interface, 45
internet, 18, 23, 44, 45, 46
Internet Connection, 18
IP address, 28
IR extender, 17, 21
IR port, 21

J

Javascript, 39

K

Kodi, 31, 32, 33, 34, 49

L

launch, ii, 11, 36, 43
LG, 5
library, 34, 41
living room, i
logo, 22

M

malfunctioning, 33
megabits, 46
microphones, 3
micro-USB, 20
Mouse, 38
movie series, 3, 34
multi-room, 5

N

Netflix, i, 1, 26, 44, 46
Network, 11, 28
new skills, 4
notification, 14, 39, 43

O

onscreen, 8, 23

P

parental guides, 11
passwords, 10
payment, 12, 45
permissions, 34
phones, 5
pictures, 4
PIN, 11
Pluto TV, 36, 37, 49
POWER, 20
power adapter, 17, 20
Preferences, 12
pressure, 22
Prime member, 45
Prime Video, i, 1
programming, 11
PS Vue, i

R

Reddit, 2
registration, 10
remote, 9, 14, 17, 22, 25, 41, 42, 43
remote control, 9, 22, 25
router, 45

S

Samsung, 5
satellite, 3, 5, 7, 14, 25
Settings, 7, 11, 12, 27, 29, 32, 34, 38, 41, 49
Setup, 18, 28
Show Box, 37, 38, 40, 49

smart home, i, 4, 14, 48, 49
smartphone, 27, 28
socket, 20
software, 19, 51
soundbar, 3, 7, 14
speakers, 15, 20
SPORTS APPS, 13
Spotify, 2, 13
stream, 40, 44, 45, 46, 47
streaming device, ii, 32, 38
streaming media, ii, 3
Stremio, 34, 35, 36, 49
Stremio ApK version, 35
subscription, 26, 44
system, 8, 9, 17, 19, 33

T

technological, ii
television, ii, 1, 2, 4, 6, 13, 14, 19, 20, 21, 32, 37, 41, 48, 49
Terrarium, 3, 26, 27, 28, 29, 30, 31, 49
third-party, 32
Toggle, 38
TV, 1, 3, i, iii, 1, 2, 3, 4, 5, 6, 7, 9, 10, 12, 13, 14, 15, 16, 17, 18, 20, 21, 22, 23, 24, 25, 26, 27, 28, 29, 30, 31, 32, 33, 34, 35, 36, 37, 39, 41, 42, 43, 44, 45, 46, 47, 48, 49

TV shows, 15, 26, 32, 34, 45, 48, 49

U

UNLOCK, 11
USB port, 15, 20

V

version, 28, 31, 33, 36
Vizio, 5
voice, i, ii, 2, 3, 4, 5, 8, 14, 17, 22, 24, 48, 49
VPN, 40

W

Walmart, 46
weather forecasts, 4
website, 33, 35
WELCOME VIDEO, 25
Wi-Fi, 9, 11, 18, 23, 44, 45
wireless, 44, 45

X

XBMC, 31
Xbox Media, 31

Y

YouTube, 2

Made in the USA
Coppell, TX
23 December 2022

90613419R00036